C00 482 235X

KU-730-653

INDIA

Anita Ganeri

W
FRANKLIN WATTS
LONDON • SYDNEY

Designer Rita Storey
Editor Sarah Ridley
Art Director Jonathan Hair
Editor-in-Chief John C. Miles
Picture research Diana Morris

First published in 2006 by Franklin Watts

Copyright © Franklin Watts 2006

Franklin Watts
338 Euston Road
London NW1 3BH

Franklin Watts Australia
Hachette Children's Books
Level 17/207 Kent Street
Sydney NSW 2000

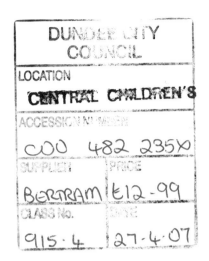

DUNDEE CITY COUNCIL

LOCATION
CENTRAL CHILDREN'S

ACCESSION NUMBER
COO 482 235X

SUPPLIER   PRICE
BERTRAM   £12.99

CLASS No.   DATE
915.4   27.4.07

All rights reserved.

A CIP catalogue record for this book
is available from the British Library.

Dewey classification number: 915.4

ISBN-10: 0 7496 6430 4
ISBN-13: 978 0 7496 6430 5

Printed in Hong Kong

Franklin Watts is a division of Hachette Children's Books.

Picture credits
Dave Amit/Reuters/Corbis: 11. AP/Empics: 5t, 26. Pallava Bagla/Corbis: 17.
BK Bangash/AP/Empics: 19. Jerry Cooke/Corbis: 24. Rob Crandall/Rex Features:
front cover tr. Dinodia: front cover tl, 22. Prakash Halvaine/AP/Empics: 16.
Mark Henley/Panos: 1, 14, 25, 27. Rod Johnson/Panos: 15.
Pawel Kopczynski/Reuters/Corbis: front cover b, 12. Rajesh Nirgude/AP/Empics: 13.
Gurinder Osan/AP/Empics: 9. Karen Robinson/Panos: 23.
Marco Simoni/Rex Features: 21. Sipa Press/Rex Features: 10, 20. Superbild/A1 Pix: 6.
Topfoto: 7, 8. Brian Vikander/Corbis: 18.

*Every attempt has been made to clear copyright. Should there be any
inadvertent omission please apply to the publisher for rectification.*

Note to parents and teachers:
Every effort has been made by the Publishers to ensure that the websites in
this book are suitable for children, that they are of the highest educational
value, and that they contain no inappropriate or offensive material.
However, because of the nature of the Internet, it is impossible to guarantee
that the contents of these sites will not be altered. We strongly advise that
Internet access is supervised by a responsible adult.

CONTENTS

#

INDIA COVERS AN AREA OF 3,287,260 SQUARE KILOMETRES, *more than a third of the size of the USA. With over one billion people, it is the second most populated country in the world, after China. Together with Bangladesh and Pakistan, India forms a subcontinent, set off from the rest of Asia by the massive Himalayan mountain range.*

India is divided into 28 states and seven union territories (areas such as islands and large cities that are part of India). The capital is New Delhi (also called Delhi), but other large and important cities include Mumbai (Bombay), Kolkata (Calcutta) and Chennai (Madras).

KNOW YOUR FACTS

India is a vast country, with a huge range of landscapes and people. It has a fast-growing economy and plays a key part in world affairs. Despite this, India is often in the news for the many problems it faces as it moves into the 21st century. They include the on-going conflict with Pakistan over the region of Kashmir, widespread poverty, a massive population, trouble between different religions and damage to the environment.

These maps show India's location in the world.

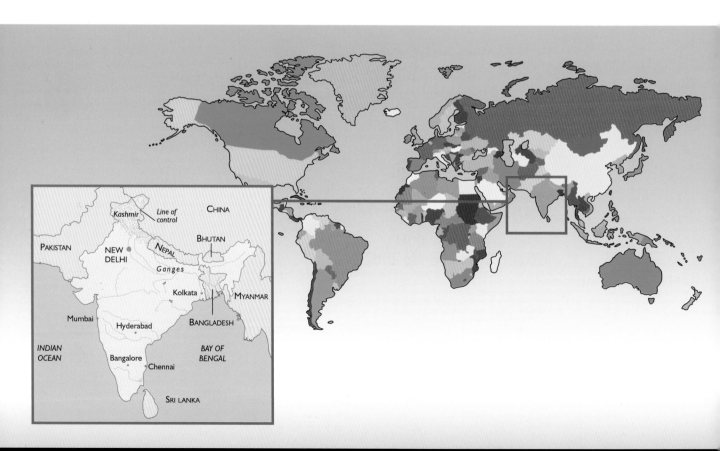

▲ Monsoon rains can cause disastrous flooding in many areas of India.

LAND AND LANDSCAPE

India has land borders with six other countries. These are Pakistan in the west and Bangladesh and Myanmar (Burma) in the east. To the north, India borders Nepal, Bhutan and China. With a long coastline, India has the Indian Ocean to the south, the Arabian Sea to the west and the Bay of Bengal to the east. India also includes the Lakshadweep Islands and Nicobar Islands.

The landscape of India ranges from snow-capped mountains to tropical rainforests, baking deserts to palm-fringed beaches. There are three main geographical regions. The first is the Himalayas, the

KNOW YOUR FACTS

The Indian climate is dominated by the monsoon, which lasts from June to September. Winds bring torrential rain, which is vital for the success of farmers' crops. If the monsoon fails, crops are ruined but particularly heavy rains can also cause disaster. In July 2005, India's largest city, Mumbai, was brought to a standstill by the worst monsoon on record. A staggering 94 centimetres of water fell in just one day. A thousand people drowned or were killed by landslides and collapsing buildings.

highest mountain range in the world, that marks India's northern boundary. The River Ganges flows from the Himalayas into the sea at the Bay of Bengal, crossing the second region, the flat, fertile Indo-Gangetic Plain. To the south is the third region, the Deccan Plateau.

INDIA'S FIRST MAJOR CIVILISATION *grew up along the banks of the River Indus in north-west India (now modern-day Pakistan) about 5,000 years ago. Two great cities, Mohenjo Daro and Harappa, formed the centres of this civilisation. Archaeologists and historians have discovered evidence of a developed and sophisticated society with organised trade and agriculture.*

In about 1500BCE, Aryan people from Central Asia began to arrive and settle in north-west India. They spread through the Indus Valley and into the valley of the River Ganges. Since then, India has been invaded many times, and ruled by many different powers.

THE MUGHAL EMPIRE

From 1526 to 1707, India was ruled by six powerful Muslim emperors, called the Mughals. The Mughal Empire was one of the most splendid ever seen, famous for its beautiful buildings, art, gardens and glittering courts. The third emperor, Akbar (ruled 1556-1605), was known for his religious tolerance and tried to treat Hindus and other non-Muslims fairly. However, the last of the great Mughals, Aurangzeb (ruled 1658-1707), was a strict Muslim. He abandoned Akbar's ideas and treated Hindus very badly.

The Taj Mahal in Agra was built by Shah Jahan, a 17th-century Mughal emperor, as a memorial to his wife.

The last British viceroy (governor) of India, Lord Louis Mountbatten, rides through crowds on Independence Day, 15 August 1947.

THE BRITISH RAJ

European traders began to arrive in India from the 15th century. In the early 17th century, the British founded the East India Company to trade in India. As they grew more powerful though, the British turned their attention from trade to gaining control of India's land. In 1858, Britain took direct control of India, marking the beginning of the British Raj (rule).

TO INDEPENDENCE AND BEYOND

Many Indians struggled to gain independence from Britain, which was finally achieved in 1947. After a period of unrest, during which many people died, India became a stable democracy.

KNOW YOUR FACTS

Towards the end of the 19th century, Indians began to speak out against British rule and to demand a greater say in the running of their country. One of their greatest leaders was Mahatma Gandhi (1869-1948). He believed that the best way to fight the British was with peaceful protest, rather than force. His non-violent campaign helped to bring about independence for India from Britain in August 1947.

Over the last 60 years, India has remained the world's largest democracy. It has had many different leaders, mostly from the Congress Party (see page 10). With its growing economy, it has recently begun to play a much larger part in world affairs.

PEOPLE OF INDIA: HINDUS AND MUSLIMS

 In 1992 Hindu extremists tore down a Muslim mosque at Ayodhya and replaced it with a Hindu temple, sparking fierce clashes.

OVER 80 PER CENT OF INDIA'S PEOPLE ARE HINDUS *and about 14 per cent are Muslims. Of the rest, about two per cent are Christians, with a similar number of Sikhs, together with smaller number of Buddhists, Jains and followers of other religions. Religion plays a hugely important part in people's lives, often determining where people live and whom they marry.*

According to Indian law, every Indian has the right to follow their religion freely. In spite of this, India is often in the news for the conflicts between its religious groups, particularly Hindus and Muslims.

GROUNDS FOR DEBATE

Many Hindus and Muslims live peacefully but extremist groups on both sides are becoming more dangerous. In 1992, Hindu extremists destroyed a mosque in Ayodhya in northern India. They believe that the town was the birthplace of the great Hindu god, Lord Rama, and that the mosque stood on top of an ancient temple. This triggered violence between Hindus and Muslims in which more than 300 people died. Why do you think religious beliefs can lead to violence?

HINDUISM AND ISLAM

Hindus follow the religion of Hinduism, one of the world's oldest faiths. It goes back at least 4,000 years to ancient India. Clay figures of deities similar to those of Hinduism have been found among the ruins of the Indus Valley cities (see page 6). The beliefs of the Indus peoples mixed with those of the later settlers, the Aryans, to form the basis of Hinduism.

Islam began in Arabia in the 7th century CE. It reached India in the 11th century when Muslim armies from Afghanistan led raids into the north west. This marked the beginning of 700 years of Muslim rule in India. Today, India is home to more Muslims than any other country, except Indonesia.

Indian police often have to deal with the after-effects of Hindu/Muslim extremist violence. This bomb blast took place in New Delhi on 30 October 2005.

RELIGIOUS TENSIONS

Many of India's religious tensions have their roots in recent history. During the struggle for independence from Britain, Muslims began to demand their own, separate country. To try to stop the growing violence between Hindus and Muslims, the British divided India in 1947 into Hindu India and Muslim Pakistan. A bloodbath followed. Millions of Hindus and Muslims were stranded on the "wrong" side of the new borders. As they tried to escape to safety, hundreds of thousands of people were massacred.

KNOW YOUR FACTS

In recent years, several Indian cities have been hit by terrorist bomb attacks. In August 2003, two huge car bombs exploded in Mumbai and in October 2005, three more bombs exploded in Delhi. Many people were killed and even more injured. It is thought that the bombings were organised by Muslim extremist groups, based in Pakistan. These groups are fighting against Indian rule in Kashmir (see pages 18-19).

INDIA BECAME A REPUBLIC IN 1950. *It is the world's largest democracy, with over 670 million voters. General elections are held every five years, with everyone over 18 allowed to vote.*

The Indian parliament has two houses – the Lok Sabha (Council of the People) and the Rajya Sabha (Council of States). The President is head of state. The Prime Minister is head of the government and governs with the help of the Council of Ministers. Each Indian state has its own chief minister.

POLITICAL PARTIES

The two largest political parties in India are the Congress Party and the Bharatiya Janata Party, or BJP, (Indian People's Party). The Congress Party was formed in 1885 to fight for Indian independence. It remained in power for most of the time from Independence until the mid-1990s.

Sonya Gandhi, leader of the Congress Party.

KNOW YOUR FACTS

Three of India's Congress prime ministers have come from the remarkable Nehru-Gandhi family. Jawaharlal Nehru (1889-1964) was India's first prime minister. He was followed by his daughter, Indira Gandhi (1917-84), who was elected three times until her assassination in 1984. Indira's son, Rajiv (1944-91), was prime minister from 1984-89. He was assassinated in 1991. In 1998, Rajiv's widow, Italian-born Sonia Gandhi (born 1946), became President of the Congress Party. She led it to victory in the 2004 elections.

In 1996, however, Congress suffered its worst ever defeat at the hands of the BJP, a party with strong Hindu views. In 1998, the BJP formed its first government.

In the 2004 general election, Congress returned to power with a surprise victory over the BJP. Congress leader, Sonia Gandhi (see box left), turned down the job of prime minister, and Manmohan Singh was sworn in as India's first Sikh leader. He announced that his aims were to reduce poverty, strengthen India's economy and establish friendlier links with India's neighbours, particularly Pakistan.

GROUNDS FOR DEBATE

Governing a country as vast and varied as India is extremely difficult but the job is made even harder by widespread corruption in almost every section of Indian society. Some people say this is because people earn very little but many rich people are also corrupt. Others say that India has such a culture of corruption that people do not see it as wrong and bribing people is often the only way of getting things done.
What do you think?

Supporters wave flags at a 2004 BJP election rally.

The new face of India: IT workers in a modern office.

IN RECENT YEARS, INDIA'S ECONOMY HAS GROWN FAST. *It is now in the top ten of the world's biggest economies and is one of the largest in Asia. India's industries include steel, chemicals, machinery, software and textiles. It has trading links with the USA, United Arab Emirates, China and Britain. But not everyone is doing well. The country is home to a quarter of the world's poorest people, and there is a massive gap between rich and poor.*

SOFTWARE SUPERPOWER

In the late 1990s, India became a top producer of computer software. Today, most of the world's software is made in India and then exported. This has had a huge effect on India's economy. Many of the world's biggest IT (information technology) companies have set up offices in India. They use highly skilled Indian workers to research and develop new products. With 150,000 software workers, the city of Bangalore is the IT capital of India but the industry is spreading all over the country.

GROUNDS FOR DEBATE

India has a sophisticated space programme. It launches its own satellites and plans to send a spacecraft to the Moon by 2007 or 2008. About £65 million has been spent on space research. Some people think that this money should have been spent on reducing poverty. Others say that space science helps the poor. For example, satellites monitoring the land can locate much-needed underground water supplies. What do you think?

CALL CENTRES IN INDIA

Many international companies, such as banks, airlines and insurance companies, have moved their call centres from their home countries to India. The centres handle phone calls from the companies' customers. There are hundreds of centres in cities such as Mumbai, Bangalore and Chennai.

Companies opening call centres in India take advantage of well-qualified workers and much lower salaries than in the west – workers may earn less than £3 a day. Even so, Indians are queuing up for the jobs. By Indian standards, this is a good wage and is double what an Indian teacher earns.

KNOW YOUR FACTS

"Bollywood" is the nickname given to India's massive film industry, the largest in the world and worth billions of pounds a year. More than 800 films are made each year, mostly in Mumbai. They are usually long and action-packed, with glamorous stars, singing and dancing. Films are made so quickly that actors sometimes work on scenes for four different films at a time. Bollywood films are watched all over the world. In India itself, an estimated 14 million people go to the cinema every day.

Posters advertising "Bollywood" films are present in most Indian cities.

THE LARGEST INDIAN CITIES ARE *Mumbai (16.4 million people), Kolkata (13.2 million), New Delhi (12.8 million), and Chennai (6.4 million), and city populations continue to grow fast. By 2020, half of all Indians may live in cities. This is partly because of India's growing population but also because many poor people are moving from the countryside to cities in search of work and better lives.*

KNOW YOUR FACTS

Even though cities are growing fast, two-thirds of Indians still live in villages in the countryside. There are estimated to be about 600,000 villages, ranging from tiny hamlets to small towns. Village life can be very hard. Many villages do not have basic services, such as clean, running water or a regular electricity supply. Villagers often live in poverty, scraping a living from farming small plots of land.

But this rapid growth is putting cities under terrible pressure. They are already overcrowded, congested with traffic and suffering shortages of basic essentials. Moreover, despite being centres of business and government, they also have some of the worst poverty in the country.

LIFE FOR THE RICH

In big cities, new western-style coffee shops, restaurants, shopping malls and housing estates are springing up. One reason for this is the growing number of middle-class Indians with good jobs in offices and call centres. Unlike their parents, they have some money to spend and can afford to buy homes and luxuries, such as cars and mobile phones.

Shanty housing contrasts starkly with modern wealthy suburbs in many large Indian cities.

 This poverty-stricken woman lives surrounded by rubbish in the Dhariva slums of Mumbai.

GROUNDS FOR DEBATE

To Hindus, cows are sacred animals; cows are allowed to roam freely on city roads among the people and traffic. This can cause problems, including road accidents and disease. A scheme launched in Delhi aims to get thousands of stray cows off the streets. The cows are fitted with computer chips, then sold at auction. Their new owners' names are listed on a database, together with the chip numbers. If a cow strays, its owner has to pay a fine. Do you think banning cows from Indian streets would solve the problem?

LIFE FOR THE POOR

In Indian cities, rich and poor live side by side but the gap between the two is huge. Many poor people hardly earn anything and live in appalling conditions in slums on the streets, along railway tracks, or near water pipelines. Their homes are makeshift shacks of mud and tin, with no toilets or running water, and often no electricity. Their lives are made even harder by the constant fear of their homes being bulldozed by the city authorities to clear land for new building. With low levels of education and work skills, it can be very difficult for people to improve their living conditions and government pledges to do more to help the poor have been criticised for being too little, too late. In India's rush to modernise, its poor are being left further and further behind.

 Tensions run high at a demonstation to protest the construction of the Narmada dam.

AS INDIA'S ECONOMY AND POPULATION GROW, *great damage is being done to the environment. Major problems include the destruction of forests for firewood, loss of farmland through soil erosion, and air and water pollution.*

Millions of poor people do not have safe drinking water. Many of them have to bathe and gather drinking water from rivers. But huge quantities of human and industrial waste are being dumped into India's rivers, turning them into filthy drains. As a result, thousands suffer from water-borne diseases, such as dysentery.

GROUNDS FOR DEBATE

Conservation groups are working hard to protect India's environment. The Narmada Bachao Andolan (Save the Narmada Movement) protests against the building of a series of dams along the Narmada river in western India. Supporters of the dam project claim that it will bring much-needed water and hydro-electric power to nearby states. Opponents argue that it will flood hundreds of villages, displacing up to one million people. Do you think that the water and electricity is worth the damage?

DIRTY AIR

Air pollution from cars, factories and power stations is a major problem in Indian cities. Delhi is one of the world's most polluted cities, largely because of the huge increase in the number of motor vehicles on the city's streets. Buses and auto-rickshaws must already use natural gas instead of petrol to cut down on harmful fumes. It is also hoped that more people will start to travel on Delhi's recently opened underground railway. This could reduce pollution by half in the next five years.

NATURAL DISASTERS

Natural disasters can have a devastating effect on India's environment. On 26 December 2004, a series of deadly tsunami waves smashed into the coast of Tamil Nadu in south-east India. Some 9,000 people died, mostly the families of poor fishermen. Tens of thousands of survivors lost everything. The fishermen were already struggling to make a living because of competition with large foreign fishing fleets. Repairing the damage is likely to take years.

 Fishing boats flung up on the shores of Tamil Nadu after the 2004 tsunami.

SINCE INDEPENDENCE, INDIA HAS BEEN *in conflict with Pakistan over the region of Kashmir. This bitter battle is still one of the major problems facing the Indian government today.*

Before Independence, parts of India were ruled by Indian princes who had to choose between joining India or Pakistan. For most, it was easy to decide, based on their location and religion. Kashmir, however, faced a dilemma. It lay very close to Pakistan and its people were mainly Muslims but its ruler was Hindu, and he chose to join India.

A peaceful scene in Kashmir, with a lake and snow-covered mountains in the background.

WAR IN KASHMIR

Almost immediately, fighting began over Kashmir. The first war between India and Pakistan lasted from 1947-49, when a ceasefire line was drawn across Kashmir. A third of Kashmir was given to Pakistan; the rest to India. But neither country was satisfied. Both claimed Kashmir and the dispute continued. In 1965, a second war broke out. A new ceasefire line, called the Line of Control, was drawn up in 1972, but fighting has continued on and off ever since.

KNOW YOUR FACTS

Kashmir lies in the far north of India on the border with Pakistan. It is officially known as Jammu and Kashmir. Nicknamed the "Switzerland of the East", it is famous for its breathtaking mountain scenery. Kashmir covers about 222,236 square kilometres and is home to some 12 million people. About two-thirds of Kashmiris are Muslims.

The first group of Pakistani Kashmiris to enter India passes through a checkpoint on the Line of Control on 7 April 2005.

PEACE TALKS

In 2001-03, heavy fighting along the Line of Control, combined with terrorist attacks in Delhi and Mumbai (see page 9), pushed India and Pakistan to the edge of war. Both sides called for peace talks, and progress has been made. In April 2005, a bus route was opened across the Line of Control for the first time since 1947. This was followed by a cricket match between the two countries in Delhi, after which the Pakistani President and Indian Prime Minister met for talks.

GROUNDS FOR DEBATE

On 8 October 2005, a massive earthquake struck Pakistani-held Kashmir. More than 73,000 people died, with a further 1,400 deaths in Indian-held Kashmir. Thousands of people were injured and millions left homeless. Faced with such a dreadful disaster, India and Pakistan began working together to help the survivors. India sent blankets, tents, food and medicines, and five crossing points were opened along the Line of Control to allow supplies through. Can you think of other natural disasters that have forced nations to work together?

 Indian nuclear missiles on show in a military parade.

TODAY, IT IS BECOMING EVEN MORE IMPORTANT *to try to solve the conflict in Kashmir. Both India and Pakistan have nuclear weapons and there is a real fear that future clashes between the two countries could lead to nuclear war.*

In May 1974, India held its first nuclear tests in the Thar Desert, in the northern state of Rajasthan, close to the border with Pakistan. A few years later, Pakistan began to develop its own nuclear programme.

KNOW YOUR FACTS

India's nuclear weapons have significant Sanskrit names. Surface-to-surface missiles are called Prithvi, which means "Earth". Two other types of missile are called Agni, after the Hindu god of fire, and Surya, after the god of the Sun. Sagarika is a missile launched by a submarine. Its name means "of the ocean".

NUCLEAR CRISIS

By the late 1990s, tensions between the two countries were running higher than ever. Then, in early May 1998, India shocked the world by carrying out a series of nuclear tests in Rajasthan. World leaders urged Pakistan not to reply. But on 28 May, Pakistan carried out five tests of its own.

INTERNATIONAL RESPONSE

Many countries were quick to criticise both India and Pakistan. They were worried that the tit-for-tat tests could lead to full-blown nuclear war. Economic sanctions were placed on both countries. This meant, for example, cutting off economic help like new bank loans.

Since 1998, India and Pakistan have come close to war several times. It seems, though, that they might have held back because of each other's nuclear threat. Both countries have continued their nuclear tests but both are under great pressure to find a peaceful solution to their problems in Kashmir.

The remote Thar Desert in Rajasthan, the site of India's nuclear tests.

GROUNDS FOR DEBATE

India has promised to use nuclear energy for peaceful purposes only. This means for generating electricity. India needs huge amounts of electricity for its growing industries and population. At present, most of this is generated by burning coal which produces lots of air pollution and contributes to global warming. Making electricity from nuclear energy is much cleaner but it also produces extremely dangerous radioactive waste which must be disposed of safely. How should India solve its energy needs?

A bride and groom at a traditional Hindu wedding.

THE LIVES OF WOMEN IN INDIA DEPEND ON MANY THINGS – *where they live, the community they belong to, whether they are rich, poor or educated. Traditionally, Indian women were expected to look after their homes, husbands and children, and most Indian women continue to fulfil this role. However, today, some women are challenging these customs. They are well-educated, have good jobs and want to be more independent.*

MARRIAGE AND DIVORCE

Most Hindu weddings are arranged by a couple's family. This custom is still very strong, even though more women are having a say in their parents' choice of husband. Until recently, very few women got divorced because of the shame this brought on their families. But the number of divorces is rising, particularly among educated women with their own jobs.

KNOW YOUR FACTS

In Hindu society, newly married women traditionally go to live with their husband's family. Most Hindu families are "joint" families, with several generations of a family living under the same roof. But some modern, working Indian women are breaking the mould. They are moving out of their parents' homes and buying their own homes with their husbands. A few women are even choosing to live on their own, though this is still not very common.

Many thousands of Indian women work in low-paid agricultural jobs, such as tea-picking.

HELPING THEMSELVES

Many poor Indian women have to work as well as running their households. In the countryside, women work on the land. In cities, they might work on building sites, stitch clothes or take in washing. Often, they work long hours for little pay and in poor conditions. But some women are helping themselves. They belong to an association called SEWA (the Self-Employed Women's Association) which was set up in 1972. SEWA gives women advice on how to get a fair deal, runs training courses and has its own bank.

KNOW YOUR FACTS

Traditionally, a bride's family is expected to give a dowry to the groom's family, even though the dowry system has been illegal since 1961. A dowry is a collection of money, jewellery, clothes and household items. Paying for a dowry puts huge pressure on poorer families. In a few cases, the groom's family gets greedy and demands more. If they do not receive it, they might treat the bride cruelly or even kill her. To tackle this tragic situation, Indian soap operas have started to feature stories about the subject. It is hoped that this will encourage women to speak up for themselves if they are badly treated. Thousands of dowry crimes go unreported or the police force does not have time to look into them.

LIFE IS VERY DIFFERENT FOR INDIAN CHILDREN *who live in the city or the countryside, or whose families are rich or poor. Children from wealthier backgrounds go to school, play with their friends and enjoy leisure time with their families. But over two-thirds of India's 400 million children live in poverty and their lives are much harder. Many of them do not have enough food and clean water or a decent home in which to grow up.*

GOING TO SCHOOL

By law, Indian children must go to school from the ages of 6 to 14. Many poor parents are very keen for their children to get a good education. The government is also trying to help poor families, for example, by providing free school meals.

GROUNDS FOR DEBATE

The official age for getting married in India is 18 years for women and 21 years for men. But in some parts of the countryside, it is traditional for girls to get married when they are as young as 10 or 11 years old. Groups campaigning against child marriages say that they lead to many problems, such as girls being left as very young widows if their husbands die. Child marriages are now illegal in India but they are a very old custom and difficult to stop. Can you think of ways the government can help to stamp out this practice?

 The quality of children's education in India depends on money. These girls are from well-off families.

However, many poor children are forced to drop out of school and start work so they do not learn to read or write. Schools also face problems such as crumbling buildings, and a lack of teachers and equipment.

STAYING HEALTHY

Children from wealthier families are usually well looked after if they fall ill. However, many poor children live in places where there are not enough doctors, and hospitals may be dirty and overcrowded. India is working hard to provide better healthcare but many children still die from diseases that could be prevented with basic medicines or vaccines. Millions of poor children also go hungry, even though India has large emergency stocks of food.

Heavy burden: a child labourer carries rocks to earn money.

KNOW YOUR FACTS

Millions of poor Indian children under the age of 15 go out to work to earn money for their struggling families. It is believed that there may be up to 100 million working children, in factories, mines, shops, fields and on building sites. The children work for long hours, for low pay, in cramped and dangerous conditions. Another 11 million homeless children live on the streets of India's big cities.

 India is gaining an ever-greater world profile. Here, Sonia Gandhi meets with US Secretary of State Condoleezza Rice.

INDIA HAS MADE GREAT PROGRESS *since it became independent in 1947. It is changing and developing fast but it faces many challenges as it moves into the 21st century. India wants to be seen as a modern country, and a world power. Yet it still struggles with huge problems.*

HELPING THE POOR

Despite India's new wealth, it is estimated that 350 million people live on less than 60 pence per day. Several new government schemes have been launched to try to tackle poverty.

KNOW YOUR FACTS

In May 2000, the billionth baby was born in India. Despite government schemes to encourage family planning, India's population continues to grow rapidly. Today, it stands at about 1.05 billion and is increasing by 1.3 million per month. At this rate, it could top two billion by 2050. Tackling the problems caused by such a massive population, such as shortages of food and water, homelessness and greater poverty, is one of the most urgent challenges facing India in the future.

They include the four-year Bharat Nirman ("Building India") project which aims to provide electricity, houses, safe drinking water and at least one phone to millions of villages across India by 2009. Another scheme aims to help villagers find employment by promising them 100 days of work a year building roads and canals.

FOREIGN POLICY

As India becomes more powerful, its relations with other countries are changing. In 2001, the USA lifted the sanctions it had placed on India in 1998 (see page 21). It has now agreed to co-operate with India over nuclear technology.

As the two biggest economies in Asia, India and China want good trading links. To improve relations, they have been trying to resolve a long-standing quarrel over their northern border. India now recognises that Tibet is part of China; China recognises Sikkim as part of India. Even more importantly, India's relations with Pakistan are better than they have been for years, and there are real signs of progress in resolving their conflict over Kashmir.

KNOW YOUR FACTS

India's booming information technology is slowly becoming available to some of its poorer people. In some locations, fishermen are using mobile phones to price up their catch before they reach port. In cities, many auto-rickshaw drivers carry phones so that customers can call for a ride. In some villages, schemes are being run to allow farmers access to the Internet. They can use it to buy grain and tools on-line, get up-to-date weather reports, and check crop prices so that they do not get cheated.

India is attempting to modernise fast but poverty means that traditional methods are often the only ones available.

5000BCE First farming settlements in western parts of India.

2500BCE The Indus Valley Civilisation, centred on the cities of Harappa and Mohenjo Daro in north-west India, is at its height.

1500BCE The Aryan people invade from Central Asia and spread through the Indus and Ganges valleys. Their religion forms the basis of Hinduism.

480BCE Siddhartha Gautama (later the Buddha) is born in north-east India.

326BCE Alexander the Great (of Macedonia) crosses the River Indus into India.

50CE Trade flourishes between India and the Roman Empire.

320–550 The Gupta Empire flourishes in India, bringing a golden age of Hinduism.

711 Arab general, Mohammad Bin Qasam, marches into the region now known as Pakistan with an army of 60,000 Muslims.

1001 Muslim ruler, Mahmud of Ghazni, leads raids into north-west India from Afghanistan.

1206 The Muslim Sultanate of Delhi is established in northern India.

1469 Guru Nanak, the founder of Sikhism, is born in north-west India.

1498 The Portuguese arrive in India (led by Vasco Da Gama).

1526 Babur, the ruler of Kabul in Afghanistan, founds the Muslim Mughal Empire in India.

1619 The English East India Company sets up its first trading post at Surat in western India.

1784 With the passing of the India Act, the British take political control of India.

1857 The First War of Independence (sometimes called the Indian Mutiny).

1858 The government of India passes directly into the hands of the British Crown.

1876 Queen Victoria is proclaimed Empress of India.

1885 The Indian National Congress is formed to fight for power to pass into Indian hands.

1906 The All India Muslim League is formed to advance Muslim political interests. It campaigns for a separate Muslim state in Pakistan.

1920 Mahatma Gandhi launches his campaign of non-violent civil disobedience against British rule.

1942–43 Congress launches the "Quit India" movement to end British rule.

1947 India gains independence from British rule but Partition creates Muslim East and West Pakistan, divided by 1,600 km of Indian territory. Millions die in the violence that follows. Jawaharlal Nehru becomes India's first Prime Minister.

1948 Mahatma Gandhi is assassinated. War breaks out between India and Pakistan over Kashmir.

1951–52 Congress wins India's first general elections under Nehru's leadership.

1962 India loses brief border war with China.

1964 Death of Jawaharlal Nehru.

1965 Second war with Pakistan over Kashmir.

1966 Nehru's daughter, Indira Gandhi, becomes Prime Minister.

1971 Third war with Pakistan, over the creation of Bangladesh (formerly East Pakistan).

1974 India explodes its first nuclear device.

1984 Indira Gandhi is assassinated by her Sikh bodyguards. Her son, Rajiv, takes over.

1991 Rajiv Gandhi is assassinated during an election campaign.

1992 Hindu extremists destroy a mosque in Ayodhya, triggering widespread Hindu-Muslim violence.

1996 Congress suffers its worst ever election defeat and the pro-Hindu BJP (Bharatiya Janata Party) becomes the largest single political party.

1998 The BJP forms a government under Prime Minister Atal Behari Vajpayee. India conducts more nuclear tests.

2000 India marks the birth of its billionth citizen.

2001 A massive earthquake hits Gujarat, western India. A terrorist squad attacks the Indian Parliament in Delhi.

2002 War between India and Pakistan looks likely as tensions mount over Kashmir.

2004 The Congress Party wins a surprise victory in the general election. Manmohan Singh is sworn in as Prime Minister. Thousands are killed when a tsunami devastates coastal communities in the south and on the Andaman and Nicobar islands.

2005 A historic bus route is opened across the Line of Control (ceasefire line) in Kashmir for the first time since 1947. India signs a nuclear co-operation deal with the USA. Mumbai records its heaviest monsoon ever, which causes widespread flooding. A massive earthquake hits Kashmir.

BASIC FACTS

LOCATION: South Asia, bordering Pakistan in the west, Bangladesh and Myanmar in the east, and Nepal, Bhutan and China to the north.

TOTAL LAND AREA: 3,287,260 sq km.

CLIMATE: India's climate varies from temperate in the north to tropical in the south, with an average summer temperature on the plains of 27^0C. In June and July, the summer monsoon brings heavy rain over much of the country.

POPULATION: 1,080,264,388 (2005 estimate).

AVERAGE AGE: 24 years.

LANGUAGES: Hindi (the national language), with 14 other official languages (Bengali, Telugu, Marathi, Tamil, Urdu, Gujarati, Malayalam, Kannada, Oriya, Punjabi, Assamese, Kashmiri, Sindhi and Sanskrit). English is the most important language for politics and business.

CURRENCY: Indian rupee (INR).

LITERACY RATE: about 60 per cent of the total population aged over 15 can read and write; 70 per cent of men over 15 can read and write, compared to 48 per cent of women (2003 estimate).

RELIGIONS: about 80 per cent of Indians are Hindus; 14 per cent are Muslims; 2 per cent are Christians; 2 per cent are Sikhs. There is also a small number of Buddhists, Jains and followers of other religions.

archaeologists People who study the past by digging up ancient sites and objects.

assassination When a public or political figure is murdered, usually by a surprise attack.

call centres Centres set up by companies such as banks where workers handle phone calls from the companies' customers.

auto-rickshaw A light, two-wheeled vehicle powered by a motor which is a common means of transport in Indian cities.

ceasefire An agreement to end a war or a period of fighting.

corruption When people give and receive bribes of money and goods in return for favours, such as special treatment.

deities Gods and goddesses.

democracy A government which is elected, or chosen, by all of a country's people.

dowry An amount of money and goods that an Indian woman's family traditionally had to give to her husband's family on the occasion of her marriage.

economy The value of a country's natural resources, industries and wealth.

emperor A single ruler who governs a group of countries or people called an empire.

exported When goods produced by a country are sold abroad.

extremist A person or group with very strong political or religious views.

general elections Elections in which the people of a country vote for that country's leaders.

Himalayas The vast mountain range which divides the Indian subcontinent from the rest of Asia are called the Himalayas. The range includes many of the world's highest mountains, including Mt Everest.

Hindus People who follow the religion of Hinduism.

independence Freedom from rule by another country or power.

monsoon The annual winds which bring torrential rain to many parts of India.

mosque A Muslim place of prayer and worship.

Mughal The Muslim rulers of India from 1526-1707.

Muslim A Muslim is someone who follows the religion of Islam.

pesticide A powerful chemical used on farmland to kill insects and other pests.

plateau A flat, raised area of land. The Deccan Plateau is in south-central India.

republic A country governed by an elected head of state called a president.

sacred Another word for holy.

sanctions Measures agreed by countries against another country that has broken international law.

Sanskit The ancient language of India which has special importance as the sacred language of Hinduism.

slums Dirty and overcrowded parts of a city containing run-down housing, poor services and often having a high crime rate.

subcontinent A large land mass that is part of a continent. The Indian subcontinent is part of the continent of Asia.

tsunami A series of vast waves usually triggered off by an underwater earthquake.

WEBSITES

http://news.bbc.co.uk/2/hi/country_profiles/default.stm
BBC country information on India.

www.cia.gov/cia/publications/factbook
US government country profiles with information on geography, people, government and economy.

http://lcweb2.loc.gov/frd/cs/cshome.html
US Library of Congress in-depth country profiles with comprehensive information about India.

www.infochange.india.org
Up-to-date information and debates on issues such as marriage, the role of women and poverty in India.

www.indiainfo.com
News, views and information about India today.

http://india.gov.in
An information website by the Indian Government with information about health, education and business.

www.hinduonline.com
http://timesofindia.indiatimes.com
www.hindustantimes.com
Indian newspapers published in English.

www.working children.org
www.endchild exploitation.org.uk
Two useful sites dealing with the issue of child labour in India and other countries.